Winnie the Pooh

Does It Float?

Pooh and his friends were looking forward to
a day filled with adventure. They were going on an expedition!
Everyone was ready to set off—but where was Tigger?

"Look out! Comin' through!" called Tigger. He bounced out of the Hundred-Acre Wood dragging something large behind him.

"What is it?" asked Pooh.

"A raft, of course!" Tigger replied, pushing it into the stream. "This here floaty boat will get us where we want to go in no time."

"Are you sure it's safe?" asked Rabbit nervously.

"Of course!" Tigger said proudly. "I made it myself!"

Once the raft was on the water, the friends climbed aboard carrying a honeypot, inner tube, a basket of strawberries, butterfly net, pail, and a big, round rock. In no time at all, they were on their way.

"Congratulations, Tigger," said Rabbit. "Your raft floats nicely, indeed."

"Thank you, Long Ears," Tigger replied. "So, where are we going on this expotition anyway?"

"I don't know," said Rabbit. "Do you, Pooh?"

"Not very far," replied Eeyore, "because our raft has decided to go its separate ways."

Rabbit looked down and saw the logs drifting apart underneath them. "Oh, dear!" he cried. "We must get to shore!"

"Land ho!" shouted Tigger. He grabbed Piglet's butterfly net and used the handle to pull the rickety craft to the bank.

The friends scrambled off just as the raft came apart completely. Everyone watched as the logs bobbed off in all directions.

"Hey, look!" shouted Roo. "Everything we brought with us is floating!"

Pooh's honeypot was floating. Tigger's inner tube was floating. Rabbit's basket of strawberries was floating. Piglet's butterfly net was floating, and Roo's pail was floating, too!

"Well, not everything we brought," Eeyore remarked.

"What do you mean?" asked Pooh.

"My lucky rock," Eeyore replied. "It's gone."

Roo scanned the water. "But where is it?" he asked.

"At the bottom of the stream, I suppose," said Eeyore. "I have a sinking feeling it's gone forever."

"Gee, that's one unlucky lucky rock," Tigger remarked.

Everyone gathered their things when they floated to shore.

"So much for our expotition," said Pooh. "What we need is a new plan."

"Let's go to my house," Roo offered. "Mama was making cookies when I left."

"An eating plan!" exclaimed Pooh with delight. "My favorite kind."

Soon they were outside the door of the tidy house—but the cookies were still in the oven.

"Why don't you bob for apples," suggested Kanga, "until the cookies are done?"

The friends filled a tub with water and began their game. One by one, everyone took a turn trying to grab an apple in his mouth. It wasn't easy! The apples bobbed this way and that. Eeyore stood back and watched.

"Hmm," thought Eeyore. "Logs float. Empty honeypots float. Inner tubes float. Strawberries float. A butterfly net floats. A tin pail floats. Apples float. I wonder...."

"Time for cookies!" Kanga called out the window. While everyone headed inside, Eeyore went around back to Kanga's vegetable bin.

He picked up a couple of potatoes in his mouth and dropped them into the washtub. They sank. Next he threw in some carrots. Down to the bottom of the tub they went.

"Why can't I get anything to float?" wondered Eeyore.

Kanga came to the door.

"What are you doing out here by yourself, Eeyore?" she asked. Then she spotted the tub. "Oh, making vegetable soup, I see! Well, come inside for cookies. You can finish later."

Inside, Kanga brought out a big plate of cookies and poured glasses of lemonade with ice.

"No ice for me," said Eeyore. "Mine always melts." He looked around the table—and noticed that everyone's ice cubes were floating in their drinks. Again, Eeyore missed out on having something that floats.

Eeyore eyed the sugar bowl.

"I bet I know something that will float," he thought. He plopped a sugar cube into his glass—and watched it sink like a stone. "I should have known that nothing can sweeten my luck," Eeyore said with a sigh.

After their snack, the friends needed something to do.

"How about I build us another raft?" Tigger said, bouncing here and there.

"No!" cried Rabbit. "Anything but that!"

"Let's go find Christopher Robin," piped up Piglet. "He always has good ideas."

Christopher Robin patted Eeyore on the head.
"Well, what do you know?" he said. "Part of *you* floats, Eeyore!"

Eeyore smiled.

"I know it's hard to believe," he said, "but right now I'm so happy, I feel lighter than air."

Christopher Robin chuckled.

"That's funny," he replied, "because your tail is lighter than water!"

Does It Float?

One of the reasons an object floats or sinks is due to how much air it contains; if an object contains enough air to make it lighter than the surrounding water, the object will float. Eeyore's tail floated because it was lighter than the water in which it was floating.

Young children learn by questioning, observing, and experimenting.

Here's a simple buoyancy experiment that will challenge children to predict, observe, and draw conclusions. In addition to this experiment, you can also collect a small number of items and, before you place each one in the water, predict whether it will sink or float. The results may surprise you!

Step 1: Fill a bucket or small washtub with water.

Step 2: Drop small rocks into the water and observe what happens.

Step 3: Place an airtight glass or plastic jar (with the lid tightly screwed on) into the water and observe if it sinks or floats.

Step 4: Place one rock into the jar. Seal and place in the bucket and observe the results. Add another rock to the jar and repeat. Continue adding rocks, one at a time, until the jar sinks. How many rocks does it take to sink the jar?